FIRST GENERATION DMUS

ANDREW COLE

AMBERLEY

First published 2017

Amberley Publishing
The Hill, Stroud
Gloucestershire, GL5 4EP

www.amberley-books.com

Copyright © Andrew Cole, 2017

The right of Andrew Cole to be identified as the
Author of this work has been asserted in accordance
with the Copyrights, Designs and Patents Act 1988.

ISBN 978 1 4456 6640 2 (print)
ISBN 978 1 4456 6641 9 (ebook)

British Library Cataloguing in Publication Data.
A catalogue record for this book is available from
the British Library.

Origination by Amberley Publishing.
Printed in the UK.

Introduction

DMUs, or Diesel Multiple Units, were introduced onto British Railways in the early part of the twentieth century, with small individual cars used for testing and evaluation by the pre-grouping companies. The largest order was by the Great Western Railway, who ordered nearly forty single cars.

These were inherited by British Rail in 1947, and an idea was formed to use DMUs to replace steam and diesel-hauled carriages on lightly used branch lines up and down the country, and also on some of the longer distance routes. The British Rail Modernisation plan of 1955 stated that nearly 5,000 individual cars were to be built and used in various formations to help eliminate steam.

British Rail were to build the cars themselves at their Derby and Swindon workshops, but demand for the units outstripped the capacity to produce them, and so private companies were also invited to build some sets.

The largest private builder was Metro-Cammell, based at Washwood Heath, Birmingham, who built over 600 cars, mostly to the Class 101 design. The Gloucester Railway Carriage & Wagon Company, Cravens of Sheffield, Wickham of Ware, Pressed Steel of Paisley and the Birmingham Railway Carriage & Wagon Company also produced large amounts of DMUs around the late 1950s.

When the Beeching Report was published, large numbers of branch lines were to be taken out of use and lifted, thus eliminating a lot of the lines that the DMUs were being built for. The decision was made to curtail the build programme.

Most of the DMUs were delivered in green livery, with 'whiskers' on the front, and these were later replaced with a yellow square. Plain blue then followed, and then an all-over white livery with a blue stripe was used when sets were refurbished. Finally, standard BR blue and grey livery was carried by most remaining vehicles. Special liveries have been carried by various cars, including the Great Western Railway chocolate and cream Class 117, the British Telecom-liveried Class 118, the South Yorkshire PTE Class 114, and the Midline-liveried Class 121.

Most of the different classes could work in multiple with each other, as most used the blue square coupling system, but there were also red triangle and white spot coupling systems used, and these units could not work with the blue square units.

Large-scale withdrawals started taking place from the 1970s onwards, with many of the smaller non-standard classes being withdrawn first. The last first generation DMUs weren't taken out of service until 2003, although Chiltern Railways and Arriva Trains Wales have used single cars in recent years.

A lot of the DMU cars were scrapped by Vic Berry of Leicester, M. C. Metals of Glasgow and Mayer Newman of Snailwell, as most of the cars contained asbestos and these companies had the facilities to dispose of them correctly. Mayer Newman used a large firing tunnel to completely burn the cars, thus getting rid of all combustible components, leaving just the bare metal to dispose of.

All in all the DMUs were a success, and achieved what they were designed to do. Plenty have entered preservation, as they are invaluable for use on quieter days, or before steam engines have been readied for service.

I have chosen some of my favourite photographs for this book, and being based in Birmingham there are plenty of shots in the Midlands, although there are shots taken from Scotland to Penzance. I have also decided to use many photographs of DMUs on depots, as I feel this maybe an area where people don't get to see. All photographs were taken with permission, and I do hope you enjoy looking through this book, and hopefully it will jog some memories.

50164, 20 September 2009
50164 (53164) *Daisy* rests at the Midland Railway Centre, Butterley. This Class 101 car was built by Metro-Cammell, Birmingham, in 1957. Towards the end of its British Rail career, this car was returned to green livery.

50266, 27 May 2016
50266 (53266) is seen preserved at Loughborough on the Great Central Railway. This car has been repainted back into BR green livery, and has an Eastern Region prefix. This Class 101 car was built by Metro-Cammell, Birmingham, in 1957.

50397, 22 April 2001
50397 (975137) is seen preserved at the Coventry Railway Centre. This Class 103 car was built by Park Royal, Stockport, in 1957. 50397 would enter departmental service as a viaduct inspection unit, which lead to it being preserved. Unfortunately it was scrapped in 2009, having moved to Swansea.

50416, 26 March 2016
50416 (975005) is seen having been superbly restored to original condition at the Llangollen Railway. This Class 109 car was built by Wickham, Ware, in 1957. This was another car that entered departmental service, as an Eastern Region General Manager's Saloon. It was originally preserved at the Chasewater Railway, before moving to Llangollen.

50619, 30 July 2016
50619 (53619) is seen preserved at Norchard on the Dean Forest Railway. This Class 108 car was built by BR at Derby in 1958 and has been beautifully restored back to as delivered condition, complete with whiskers on the front.

50861, 31 July 1982
50861 (53861) departs Birmingham New Street carrying BR blue and grey livery, complete with WM logo on the side. This Class 116 car was built by BR at Derby in 1958 and would eventually be scrapped by Mayer Newman, Snailwell, in 1988.

50933, 20 July 2016
50933 (53933) stands at Bewdley on the Severn Valley Railway, having been restored back to as delivered condition. This Class 108 car was built by BR at Derby in 1960. These units are ideal on preserved lines for use on quiet days when steam locos aren't needed.

50971, 14 May 2016
50971 (53971) is seen at Bodiam on the Kent & East Sussex Railway having arrived from Tenterden. This Class 108 car was built by BR at Derby in 1959.

51017, 5 September 1998
51017 is seen preserved at Bo'ness on the Bo'ness & Kinneil Railway. This Class 126 car was built by BR at Swindon in 1959. These units were used in Scotland on Glasgow to Ayr services, and this car carries a gangway end to couple to other sets; despite being sealed up in this shot, it has since been reinstated.

51043, 5 September 1998
51043 stands in the yard at Bo'ness on the Bo'ness & Kinneil Railway. This Class 126 car was built by BR at Swindon in 1959, and was withdrawn for preservation in 1983. This class of units carried the unusual white spot multiple working system, with most DMUs being blue square.

51077, 4 January 1986
51077 is seen stabled at Tyseley carriage sidings while carrying BR blue and grey livery. This Class 119 car was built by the Gloucester Railway Carriage & Wagon Company in 1959, and spent all its life based on the Western Region. At the time it was allocated to Bristol Bath Road, and still retains a First Class section. 51077 was scrapped by Vic Berry, Leicester, in 1990.

51118, 21 November 2015
51118 is seen preserved at the Midland Railway Centre, Butterley. This Class 100 car was built by the Gloucester Railway Carriage & Wagon Company in 1957. 51118 was saved for preservation as long ago as 1972, initially by the North Yorkshire Moors Railway. Hopefully this car will be restored to working condition.

51141, 8 February 1986
51141 stands in the snow at Tyseley carriage sidings, having worked to Birmingham from Cardiff. This Class 116 car was built by BR at Derby in 1958 and spent all its working life, except for a few months when allocated to Tyseley, based on the Western Region. 51141 carries a Welsh dragon on the front, and was scrapped by M. C. Metals, Glasgow, in 1993.

51151, 21 November 2015
51151 stands at Ruddington on the Great Central Railway, having been preserved and repainted back to green livery, complete with yellow front end. This Class 116 car was built by BR at Derby in 1958 and is one of just six Class 116 cars in preservation.

51179, 21 May 1996

51179 is seen ready to depart from Llandudno with a working to Holyhead. This Class 101 car was built by Metro-Cammell, Birmingham, in 1958 and was refurbished in 1991, including a repaint into Regional Railways livery. 51179 would be scrapped at Immingham Rail Freight Terminal in 2006.

51187, 29 October 1995

51187 arrives at Glasgow Central carrying Strathclyde orange and black livery. This Class 101 car was built by Metro-Cammell, Birmingham, in 1958, and was another car refurbished in the early 1990s. The Scottish-based refurbished units carried Strathclyde livery, rather then Regional Railways livery. This car was eventually preserved by the Cambrian Railway Trust, Oswestry.

51189, 21 June 1986

51189 stands in the sunshine at Tyseley carriage sidings carrying BR blue and grey livery. This Class 101 car was built by Metro-Cammell, Birmingham, in 1958, and had just been transferred to Tyseley from Chester. 51189 would find a home at the Keighley & Worth Valley Railway.

51194, 4 January 1986

51194 is seen stabled on Tyseley Depot carrying BR blue and grey livery. This Class 101 car was built by Metro-Cammell, Birmingham, in 1958, and would be scrapped by Mayer Newman, Snailwell, in 1991. This scrapyard used to put individual cars through a firing tunnel to completely burn away everything except the metal, which was then cut up.

51205, 7 February 1988
51205 is seen on Tyseley carriage sidings carrying BR blue and grey livery. This Class 101 car was built by Metro-Cammell, Birmingham, in 1958, and was passing through Tyseley, having been transferred from Heaton, Newcastle, to Laira, Plymouth. 51205 would be preserved by the Cambrian Railway Trust, Oswestry.

51228, 20 July 2006
51228 is seen making a station call at Weybourne on the North Norfolk Railway. This Class 101 car was built by Metro-Cammell, Birmingham, in 1958, and spent all of its working life in Scotland, until being refurbished in 1990 when it moved to Tyseley. It is seen carrying all-over blue livery.

51230, 24 February 1987
51230 arrives at Peterborough with a working to Cambridge. This Class 101 car was built by Metro-Cammell, Birmingham, in 1958, and was allocated to Cambridge when seen at Peterborough. 51230 would eventually be scrapped by J. T. Landscapes, Caerwent, in 2004.

51250, 29 May 1988
51250 stands at Saltburn carrying BR blue and grey livery. This Class 101 car was built by Metro-Cammell, Birmingham, in 1958, and had not long been transferred to the North East from Ayr, and still retains its 101 set number on the front. 51250 was scrapped by Mayer Newman, Snailwell, in 1990.

51271, 28 July 1984
51271 is seen at Doncaster Works during the open day in 1984 carrying plain blue livery. This Class 105 car was built by Cravens, Sheffield, in 1958, and would be scrapped by Vic Berry, Leicester, in 1987.

51272, 22 February 1986
51272 stands at Tyseley carriage sidings carrying plain blue livery. This Class 105 car was built by Cravens, Sheffield, in 1958, and was allocated to Cambridge at the time. 51272 would be withdrawn four months later, and would be scrapped by Mayer Newman, Snailwell, in 1987.

51314, 26 December 1994
51314 spends Christmas 1994 condemned at Tyseley carriage sidings. This Class 118 car was built by the Birmingham Railway Carriage & Wagon Company in 1960, and would be scrapped by M. C. Metals, Glasgow, in 1995. Tyseley carriage sidings has two separate areas, with the carriage sidings and main depot separated by the Railway Museum.

51317, 10 August 1987
51317 is seen stabled at Laira Depot, Plymouth, carrying an advert for British Telecom. This Class 118 car was built by the Birmingham Railway Carriage & Wagon Company in 1960 and would be scrapped by Mayer Newman, Snailwell, in 1989 still carrying this advert livery.

51344, 7 December 1985
51344 is seen stabled at Tyseley carrying a fresh coat of BR blue and grey livery. This Class 117 car was built by Pressed Steel, Paisley, in 1960, and was allocated to Reading at the time, and would be scrapped by M. C. Metals, Glasgow, in 1999.

51345, 31 August 1996
51345 is seen condemned at Springburn Works, Glasgow, waiting entry to the M. C. Metals yard for final scrapping. This Class 117 car was built by Pressed Steel, Paisley, in 1960, and would be cut up two months later.

51348, 26 December 1985
51348 spends Christmas 1985 stabled at Tyseley carriage sidings. This Class 117 car was built by Pressed Steel, Paisley, in 1960, and was allocated to Bristol Bath Road at the time. 51348 would be scrapped by Booth Roe Metals, Rotherham, in 1992.

51349, 22 August 1987
51349 is seen stabled at its home depot of Reading while carrying BR blue and grey livery. This Class 117 car was built by Pressed Steel, Paisley, in 1960, and would be scrapped by M. C. Metals, Glasgow, in 1995.

51349, 22 February 1988

51349 passes Washwood Heath on its way from refurbishment at Doncaster Works back to Reading. A repaint into Network South East livery was part of the refurbishment. These moves were a regular sight at this time, and the two-car set attached was included in case of failure.

51354, 29 May 2016

51354 is seen at Peak Rail having been beautifully restored into as-built condition, complete with whiskers on the front. This Class 117 car was built by Pressed Steel, Paisley, in 1960.

51359, 5 October 1995
51359 arrives at Clapham Junction with a working from Willesden Junction while carrying Network South East livery. This Class 117 car was built by Pressed Steel, Paisley, in 1960 and was preserved by the Northampton & Lamport Railway, but was stripped for spares before being scrapped in 2012 by C. F. Booth, Rotherham.

51360, 21 August 2016
51360 is seen preserved at the Gloucestershire & Warwickshire Railway, having been restored carrying plain blue livery. This Class 117 car was built by Pressed Steel, Paisley, in 1960 and has been based at various preserved sites following withdrawal from BR.

51363, 21 August 2016
51363 is seen at Toddington on the Gloucestershire & Warwickshire Railway while on a shuttle service to Winchcombe. This Class 117 car was built by Pressed Steel, Paisley, in 1960 and looks superb restored as a three-car unit.

51367, 26 December 1985
51367 is seen stabled at Tyseley carriage sidings carrying BR blue and grey livery. This Class 117 car was built by Pressed Steel, Paisley, in 1960 and was allocated to Bristol Bath Road at the time. 51367 would eventually be preserved at the Strathspey Railway, Aviemore.

51375, 12 August 1995
51375 (977992) is seen stabled at Long Rock Depot, Penzance, carrying Network South East livery. This Class 117 car was built by Pressed Steel, Paisley, in 1960 and would eventually be converted to a sandite car for Chiltern Railways. As part of the conversion, the cab was removed, and water tanks were fitted throughout.

51391, 14 March 1987
51391 is seen stabled at Tyseley carriage sidings having been split from the other vehicles in the set. This Class 117 car was built by Pressed Steel, Paisley, in 1960 and is seen being returned to Reading Depot following collision damage repairs at Doncaster Works. 51391 would be scrapped by M. C. Metals, Glasgow, in 1995.

51394, 3 September 1994

51394 is seen undergoing repairs inside Springburn Works, Glasgow, while carrying Regional Railways livery. This Class 117 car was built by Pressed Steel, Paisley, in 1960 and would be scrapped by M. C. Metals, Glasgow, in 1998.

51395, 20 September 2009

51395 is seen preserved at the Midland Railway Centre, Butterley, carrying Regional Railways livery, but with Scotrail logos. This Class 117 car was built by Pressed Steel, Paisley, in 1960 and, despite being preserved, it would be sold to the Dean Forest Railway to be scrapped in 2012.

51396, 13 September 1986
51396 is seen at Tyseley Depot on its way from Doncaster Works to Reading following
refurbishment and repaint into Network South East livery. This Class 117 car was
built by Pressed Steel, Paisley, in 1960 and has been preserved at Peak Rail, Matlock.

51400, 7 September 2006
51400 arrives at Ropley on the Mid Hants Railway while carrying BR green livery.
This Class 117 car was built by Pressed Steel, Paisley, in 1960 and has since moved to
the Wensleydale Railway.

51401, 2 November 1990

51401 departs West Drayton while heading for London Paddington, carrying Network South East livery. This Class 117 car was built by Pressed Steel, Paisley, in 1960 and these units were replaced on this route by the Class 165s. 51401 can today be found at the Gwili Railway.

51402, 17 September 2015

51402 is seen stabled at Boat of Garten on the Strathspey Railway having been restored to BR green livery, complete with Scottish Region prefix. This Class 117 car was built by Pressed Steel, Paisley, in 1960.

51405, 4 April 1995
51405 is seen departing Kensington Olympia carrying Network South East livery
with a working from Clapham Junction to Willesden Junction. Today these services
are operated by London Overground Class 378 electric units. This Class 117 car was
built by Pressed Steel, Paisley, in 1960 and has been preserved at the Gloucestershire &
Warwickshire Railway.

51408, 22 August 1987
51408 is seen stabled at its home depot of Reading carrying Network South East
livery. This Class 117 car was built by Pressed Steel, Paisley, in 1960 and would be
scrapped by C. F. Booth, Rotherham, in 2009.

51410, 18 January 1986
51410 arrives at Birmingham New Street, having just been repainted in connection with the GWR 150 celebrations, and looks superb in chocolate and cream livery. This set was allocated to Bristol Bath Road at the time, but would eventually be reallocated to Tyseley. This Class 117 car was built by Pressed Steel, Paisley, in 1960 and would be scrapped by M. C. Metals, Glasgow, in 1996, having suffered fire damage.

51414, 8 March 1986
51414 is seen stabled at Tyseley carriage sidings carrying BR blue and grey livery. This set was allocated to Bristol Bath Road at the time, and the centre car still retains its First Class section. This Class 117 car was built by Pressed Steel, Paisley, in 1960 and was scrapped by Gwent Demolition, Margam, in 1996.

51442, 20 May 1996
51442 is seen at Chester carrying Regional Railways livery, having arrived from Manchester Piccadilly. This Class 101 car was built by Metro-Cammell, Birmingham, in 1959 and was scrapped by Sims Metals, Cardiff, in 2003.

51457, 14 May 1988
51457 is seen stabled alongside the factory at Tyseley Depot. It had been transferred down from Eastfield the week before, but would only be in use in the Midlands for one month before being withdrawn. It was scrapped by Vic Berry, Leicester, in 1989.

51485, 25 May 1998
51485 is seen preserved at Bury on the East Lancashire Railway. This Class 105 car was built by Cravens, Sheffield, in 1959. 51485 was withdrawn as long ago as 1981, and hopefully a return to working order is not too far away.

51495, 27 February 1988
51495 is seen stabled outside the main factory at Tyseley Depot. This Class 101 car was built by Metro-Cammell, Birmingham, in 1959. Despite the smart appearance, this car was actually withdrawn and was allocated to Neville Hill, Leeds, at the time. It would be scrapped by Mayer Newman, Snailwell, in 1990.

51503, 1 September 1987
51503 is seen waiting to depart Leeds Station and is seen complete with WYPTE MetroTrain logos. This Class 101 car was built by Metro-Cammell, Birmingham, in 1959 and has since been preserved at the Mid Norfolk Railway.

51508, 7 June 1992
51508 rests outside the main depot at Tyseley carrying BR blue and grey livery. This Class 101 car was built by Metro-Cammell, Birmingham, in 1959 and in the photo had just been transferred to Tyseley from Norwich. 51508 would be scrapped by M. C. Metals, Glasgow, in 1993.

51511, 12 April 1986
51511 is seen stabled at Tyseley carriage sidings while carrying BR blue and grey livery, having worked up from Cardiff. This Class 101 car was built by Metro-Cammell, Birmingham, in 1959 and would be preserved at the North Yorkshire Moors Railway.

51511, 25 February 1993
51511 is seen departing Crewe with a working to Nottingham while carrying unbranded Strathclyde PTE orange and black livery. These units were based at Tyseley for a short time following refurbishment before heading for Scotland. This Class 101 car was built by Metro-Cammell, Birmingham, in 1959 and was preserved at the North Yorkshire Moors Railway.

51530, 10 August 1992
51530 is seen waiting to depart from Plymouth with a working to Gunnislake. This
Class 101 car was built by Metro-Cammell, Birmingham, in 1959 and still retains a
First Class section. 51530 would be scrapped by M. C. Metals, Glasgow, in 1993.

51566, 18 June 2006
51566 is seen preserved at Peak Rail, Matlock, carrying BR blue and grey livery,
complete with white cab roof and non-standard headlight. This Class 108 car was
built BR at Derby in 1959. Today 51566 can be found at the Dean Forest Railway.

51571, 29 March 2016
51571 is seen preserved at Tenterden on the Kent & East Sussex Railway, having been restored to original condition. This Class 108 car was built by BR at Derby in 1960.

51575, 24 February 1987
51575 departs from Peterborough having been converted to Parcels use. This Class 120 car was built by BR at Swindon in 1961 and was only in Parcels use for twelve months before being withdrawn. It would be scrapped by Mayer Newman, Snailwell, in 1988.

51591, 21 November 2015
51591 (55966) is seen preserved at the Midland Railway Centre, Butterley. This Class 127 car was built by BR at Derby in 1959, and when it was withdrawn it was claimed by the NRM, York. It later passed back to BR for conversion to a Parcels unit, being rebuilt with roller doors and renumbered 55966. At Butterley it has been rebuilt back to passenger use.

51657, 28 June 1987
51657 is seen stabled at Tyseley carriage sidings on its way back to Marylebone from Doncaster Works, having collected a refurbished centre car. This Class 115 car was built by BR at Derby in 1960, and would be scrapped by Gwent Demolition, Margam, in 1995.

51659, 3 March 1991
51659 rests inside Marylebone Depot, London, while carrying Network South East livery. The Class 165s replaced these units on this route to Aylesbury, and when they were replaced, the depot was closed and demolished. This Class 115 car was built by BR at Derby in 1960, and was scrapped by Booth Roe Metals, Rotherham, in 1992.

51823, 1 June 1988
51823 is seen at Leeds Station carrying BR blue and grey livery. This Class 110 car was built by the Birmingham Railway Carriage & Wagon Company in 1961, and would be scrapped by Mayer Newman, Snailwell, in 1990.

51827, 10 August 1988
51827 is seen at Leeds carrying BR blue and grey livery, complete with WYPTE
MetroTrain logos. This Class 110 car was built by the Birmingham Railway
Carriage & Wagon Company in 1961, and would be scrapped by Mayer Newman,
Snailwell, in 1990.

51876, 7 June 1987
51876 is seen stabled on Tyseley Depot carrying BR blue and grey livery, and has had
a WM logo applied to the front end. This Class 115 car was built by BR at Derby in
1960, and would be scrapped by Booth Roe Metals, Rotherham, in 1992.

51879, 14 June 1986

51879 is seen being shunted around Tyseley Depot by the resident Class 08 pilot. This Class 115 car was built by BR at Derby in 1960, and despite being at the Midlands depot, this car was never allocated to Tyseley. At the time it was based at Marylebone, and would be further transferred to Bletchley and Old Oak Common before being withdrawn and then scrapped by Gwent Demolition, Margam, in 1993.

51884, 26 April 1987

51884 is seen inside the factory at Tyseley undergoing repairs. This Class 115 car was built by BR at Derby in 1960 and at the time was instantly recognisable by having the domino style headcode – one of the few DMU cars to do so. 51884 would be scrapped by M. C. Metals, Glasgow, in 1993.

51893, 20 October 1990
51893 is seen at London Marylebone carrying Network South East livery. This Class 115 car was built by BR at Derby in 1960, and would be scrapped by Gwent Demolition, Margam, in 1992.

51910, 3 May 1986
51910 is seen stabled at Tyseley carriage sidings carrying BR blue and grey livery, complete with GMPTE logo. This Class 108 car was built by BR at Derby in 1960. 51910 would meet an unfortunate end; ending up in the River Towy after the bridge it was travelling on collapsed into the river. Four people died in the accident, including the driver, and 51910 would be scrapped by a private contractor at Pantyffynon in 1988.

51927, 20 June 1987
51927 is seen stabled on Tyseley Depot carrying BR blue and grey livery. This Class 108 car was built by BR at Derby in 1960, and had only been based at Tyseley for one month following transfer from Buxton. 51927 would be scrapped by Gwent Demolition, Margam, in 1992.

51932, 1 August 1987
51932 (977840) rests at Tyseley Depot carrying BR blue and grey livery, and also sports an unusual Midline logo. This Class 108 car was built by BR at Derby in 1960, and following withdrawal it was taken into departmental service as a sandite car. When this role was finished it was scrapped by Gwent Demolition, Margam, in 1995.

51934, 28 November 1987
51934 is seen at Tyseley Depot showing signs of the severe fire damage it received at Tipton, which resulted in its withdrawal. This Class 108 car was built by BR at Derby in 1960, and would be scrapped by a private contractor at Tyseley in 1988.

51936, 28 June 1987
51936 is seen stabled at Tyseley carriage sidings carrying BR blue and grey livery. This Class 108 car was built by BR at Derby in 1960 and had not long been transferred to Tyseley from Buxton. It was later transferred away to Eastfield, and would be scrapped by Gwent Demolition, Margam, in 1992.

51941, 20 July 2016
51941 is seen having been beautifully restored to original condition at Bewdley on the
Severn Valley Railway. This Class 108 car was built by BR at Derby in 1960.

51943, 15 February 1988
51943 passes through Washwood Heath carrying BR blue and grey livery, complete
with Buxton-style white cab roof. This Class 108 car was built by BR at Derby in
1960 and would be scrapped by M. C. Metals, Glasgow, in 1993.

51962, 24 August 1983
51962 arrives at Doncaster Station with a Trans-Pennine working. This Class 124 car was built by BR at Swindon in 1960 and would be scrapped by Mayer Newman, Snailwell, in 1984. In my opinion these were some of the best looking first generation DMU cars built.

51966, 20 April 1984
51966 departs Doncaster Station with a Trans-Pennine working heading towards Sheffield. This Class 124 car was built by BR at Swindon in 1960, and would be scrapped, like the majority of the class, by Mayer Newman, Snailwell, in 1985.

52021, 25 May 1986

52021 is seen in the yard at St Rollox Works, Glasgow, having just been released from overhaul, including a repaint into Strathclyde·PTE orange and black livery. This Class 107 car was built by BR at Derby in 1961 and would be scrapped by M. C. Metals, Glasgow, in 1992.

52046, 12 April 1986

52046 (977819) is seen stabled at Tyseley carriage sidings carrying BR blue and grey livery. This Class 108 car was built by BR at Derby in 1960, and following withdrawal it was taken into departmental use as a sandite car. When it had finished in this role, it was scrapped by Booth Roe Metals, Rotherham, in 1995.

52047, 11 October 1986
52047 (977841) is seen stabled at Tyseley carriage sidings having just been released
from works overhaul, including a repaint. This Class 108 car was built by BR at
Derby in 1960, and was based at Newton Heath at the time, so it is a mystery as to
why it was on Tyseley. At this time, almost any type of DMU car from any depot could
be found at Tyseley.

52057, 16 May 1987
52057 is seen stabled at Tyseley Depot carrying BR blue and grey livery, displaying
Blake Street in the blind, which is on the Cross City North line. This Class 108 car
was built by BR at Derby in 1960, and had just transferred down from Newton Heath
Depot. It would be scrapped by Gwent Demolition, Margam, in 1992.

52062, 26 March 2016
52062 is seen preserved at the Telford Steam Railway carrying an attractive maroon and cream livery. This Class 108 car was built by BR at Derby in 1961, and had been withdrawn from Tyseley in 1991.

52069, 20 April 1984
52069 departs Doncaster Station unusually displaying red tail lights. This Class 110 car was built by the Birmingham Railway Carriage & Wagon Company in 1961 and would be scrapped by Mayer Newman, Snailwell, in 1990.

52103, 24 August 1983

52103 is seen departing Doncaster with a Trans-Pennine working. This Class 123 car was built by BR at Swindon in 1963, and this view shows the gangway end of the set. None of this class were preserved, and 52103 was scrapped by Mayer Newman, Snailwell, in 1984.

53021, 2 April 1988

53021 (50021) is seen stabled outside the factory at Tyseley Depot carrying BR blue and grey livery, complete with red bufferbeam and Midline branding. This Class 114 car was built by BR at Derby in 1957 and would be scrapped by Mayer Newman, Snailwell, in 1991.

53027, 26 December 1987
53027 (50027) rests on Tyseley carriage sidings having been converted to Parcels use. This Class 114 car was built by BR at Derby in 1957 and was scrapped by Mayer Newman, Snailwell, in 1991.

53030, 20 May 1989
53030 (50030) is seen inside Tyseley Depot having been withdrawn the week previous, and has been lifted so its bogies can be removed. This Class 114 car was built by BR at Derby in 1957 and would be scrapped by M. C. Metals, Glasgow, in 1995.

53037, 3 April 1985
53037 (50037) arrives at Nuneaton with a working towards East Anglia. These units were replaced on this route by brand-new Class 156 units. This Class 114 car was built by BR at Derby in 1957 and was scrapped by Mayer Newman, Snailwell, in 1991.

53055, 4 January 1986
53055 (50055) rests at Tyseley carriage sidings carrying BR blue and grey livery, but with the addition of black windscreen surrounds and the grey continues round the front. This Class 116 car was built by BR at Derby in 1957 and was scrapped by M. C. Metals, Glasgow, in 1995.

53082, 7 March 1987
53082 (50082) is seen in the snow at Tyseley Depot carrying BR blue and grey livery. This Class 116 car was built by BR at Derby in 1957 and was scrapped by Mayer Newman, Snailwell, in 1991.

53116, 26 December 1994
53116 (50116) spends Christmas 1994 stabled at Tyseley Depot. By this time Tyseley were coupling any cars together to make serviceable sets, hence the Network South East centre car. This Class 116 car was built by BR at Derby in 1957 and would be withdrawn six months after being seen, to be scrapped by M. C. Metals, Glasgow, in 1995.

53117, 3 December 1988
53117 (50117) stands condemned at Tyseley Depot. This had been withdrawn from Newton Heath Depot, and was merely passing through Tyseley on its way to Vic Berry, Leicester, for scrapping. This Class 116 car was built by BR at Derby in 1957 and was scrapped in 1989.

53129, 14 December 1985
53129 (50129) is seen stabled on Tyseley carriage sidings carrying BR blue and grey livery, complete with Welsh dragon and Valley Train logos. 53129 was never allocated to Tyseley, transferring straight from Cardiff to Newton Heath prior to withdrawal. This Class 116 car was built by BR at Derby in 1957 and would be scrapped by Vic Berry, Leicester, in 1988.

53159, 4 June 1988
53159 (50159) is seen stored at Tyseley Depot carrying BR blue and grey livery. This
was a lifelong Scottish Region car until transfer to Neville Hill in 1987. 53159 was
another car that turned up at Tyseley, but was never allocated to the depot. This
Class 101 car was built by Metro-Cammell, Birmingham, in 1956 and would be
scrapped by Mayer Newman, Snailwell, in 1990.

53160, 12 July 1992
53160 (50160) is seen at Doncaster Works awaiting refurbishment while still carrying
Strathclyde PTE orange and black livery. This would emerge carrying Regional
Railways livery, but would soon be painted into BR green livery. This Class 101 car
was built by Metro-Cammell, Birmingham, in 1956 and was preserved at the Midland
Railway Centre, Butterley.

53160, 7 August 1996
53160 (50160) stands at Crewe with a working to Chester, having been beautifully repainted into BR green livery. This Class 101 car was built by Metro-Cammell, Birmingham, in 1956 and was preserved at the Midland Railway Centre, Butterley.

53170, 20 September 2009
53170 (50170) is seen preserved at the Midland Railway Centre, Butterley, while carrying a unique Strathclyde Passenger Transport livery of blue with a yellow and orange stripe. There was only one two-car set that carried this livery. This Class 101 car was built by Metro-Cammell, Birmingham, in 1957 and today can be found at the Ecclesbourne Valley Railway.

53177, 25 February 1993
53177 (50177) departs Crewe for Nottingham while carrying unbranded Strathclyde orange and black livery. Following refurbishment some of the Scottish-based Class 101 sets were used by Tyseley and Longsight before heading to Scotland. This Class 101 car was built by Metro-Cammell, Birmingham, in 1957 and was scrapped by Sims Metals, Beeston, in 2003.

53178, 29 May 1988
53178 (50178) is seen waiting to depart from Saltburn Station while carrying BR blue and grey livery. This Class 101 car was built by Metro-Cammell, Birmingham, in 1957. It would be withdrawn five months later and scrapped by Mayer Newman, Snailwell, in 1989.

53189, 25 May 1986
53189 (50189) is seen inside St Rollox Works, Glasgow, undergoing overhaul, including a repaint into BR blue and grey livery. This Class 101 car was built by Metro-Cammell, Birmingham, in 1957 and would be scrapped by M. C. Metals, Glasgow, in 1993.

53200, 10 August 1992
53200 (50200, 977901) is seen at Gunnislake having arrived from Plymouth while carrying BR blue and grey livery. 53200 was taken into departmental service following withdrawal and used on sandite and route-learning duties. This Class 101 car was built by Metro-Cammell, Birmingham, in 1957 and was scrapped at Immingham Rail Freight Terminal in 2003.

53211, 26 May 1998
53211 (50211) arrives at Chester with a working from Manchester Piccadilly while carrying Regional Railways livery. This view shows the problems of slam door stock, with the doors being able to be opened while the train is still moving. This Class 101 car was built by Metro-Cammell, Birmingham, in 1957 and was scrapped by J. T. Landscapes, Caerwent, in 2004.

53219, 15 May 1988
53219 (50219) is seen stabled at Tyseley carriage sidings carrying BR blue and grey livery, complete with Tyne and Wear PTE logo. This car was only allocated to Tyseley for four months before moving to Cardiff Canton. This Class 101 car was built by Metro-Cammell, Birmingham, in 1957 and was scrapped by Vic Berry, Leicester, in 1989.

53253, 18 June 2006

53253 (50253) stands preserved at the Midland Railway Centre, Butterley, among many other preserved DMU cars. 53253 carries a unique Strathclyde Passenger Transport blue livery and was part of the only two-car set to carry this livery. This Class 101 car was built by Metro-Cammell, Birmingham, in 1957 and can today be found at the Ecclesbourne Valley Railway.

53309, 3 May 1986

53309 (50309) rests at Tyseley carriage sidings carrying BR blue and grey livery, and also a Cardiff set number on the cab front. This Class 101 car was built by Metro-Cammell, Birmingham, in 1958 and was scrapped by Vic Berry, Leicester, in 1989, having been withdrawn with collision damage.

53311, 23 April 1996

53311 (50311) arrives at Chester while still carrying Network South East livery. At the time this was one of the last un-refurbished sets still in use, and was not withdrawn until 2000. This Class 101 car was built by Metro-Cammell, Birmingham, in 1958 and would be scrapped by J. T. Landscapes, Caerwent, in 2004.

53317, 16 January 1988

53317 (50317) is seen on the wheel lathe inside Tyseley Depot while carrying BR blue and grey livery. At the time this car was allocated to Chester and was visiting for tyre-turning . This Class 101 car was built by Metro-Cammell, Birmingham, in 1958 and would be scrapped by Vic Berry, Leicester, in 1990.

53322, 28 June 1987

53322 (50322) is seen stabled on Tyseley carriage sidings carrying BR blue and grey livery as part of a three-car set. It had been transferred to Tyseley from Newton Heath and would only stay at Tyseley for one month before being transferred to Reading. This Class 101 car was built by Metro-Cammell, Birmingham, in 1958 and would be scrapped by J. T. Landscapes, Caerwent, in 2004.

53322 and 54056, 22 April 1996

53322 (50322) and 54056 (56056) are seen side by side at Chester carrying Network South East and Regional Railways livery respectively. Both Class 101 cars were built by Metro-Cammell, Birmingham – 53322 in 1958 and 54056 in 1957 – and both have been scrapped; 53322 by J. T. Landscapes, Caerwent, in 2004, while 54056 was scrapped by C. F. Booth, Rotherham, in 2006.

53333, 16 May 1987

53333 (50333) is seen stabled on Tyseley Depot among many other First Generation DMUs. This was another car to only spend one month at Tyseley before being transferred away to Reading. This Class 101 car was built by Metro-Cammell, Birmingham, in 1958 and was scrapped by M. C. Metals, Glasgow, in 1993.

53355, 11 October 1986

53355 (50355) is seen stored at Tyseley carriage sidings carrying plain blue livery, and is part of a three-car set, along with 59153 and 53812. At the time, 53355 and 53812 were to be the last of their type in BR passenger service. This Class 100 car was built by the Gloucester Railway Carriage & Wagon Company in 1957 and would be scrapped by Vic Berry, Leicester, in 1990.

53368, 10 August 1988
53368 (50368) is seen at Leeds having been converted to Parcels use, and carries plain
blue livery, complete with Red Star Parcels logos. This Class 105 car was built by
Cravens, Sheffield, in 1957 and was scrapped by Mayer Newman, Snailwell, in 1989.

53427, 21 April 1987
53427 (50427) arrives at Leeds carrying plain blue livery as part of a two-car set. This
Class 104 car was built by the Birmingham Railway Carriage & Wagon Company in
1957, and was scrapped by Vic Berry, Leicester, in 1989.

53429, 7 December 1985

53429 (50429) rests at Tyseley carriage sidings carrying plain blue livery, but with Buxton-style white cab roof and black windscreen surrounds. This Class 104 car was built by the Birmingham Railway Carriage & Wagon Company in 1957 and was scrapped by M. C. Metals, Glasgow, in 1993.

53456, 18 April 1987

53456 (50456) is seen stabled at Tyseley Depot while its partner had been uncoupled and was on the wheel lathe. 53456 was allocated to Buxton at the time, and was visiting Tyseley for tyre-turning . This Class 104 car was built by the Birmingham Railway Carriage & Wagon Company in 1957, and was scrapped by Vic Berry, Leicester, in 1988.

53461, 25 May 1986

53461 (50461) is seen stabled at Corkerhill Depot, Glasgow, while carrying BR blue and grey livery. This Class 104 car was built by the Birmingham Railway Carriage & Wagon Company in 1957 and was scrapped by Vic Berry, Leicester, in 1987.

53511, 11 June 1988

53511 (50511) is seen carrying plain blue livery while on the wheel lathe at Tyseley Depot. 53511 was allocated to Newton Heath at the time, and was visiting Tyseley for tyre-turning . This Class 104 car was built by the Birmingham Railway Carriage & Wagon Company in 1957 and would be scrapped by Vic Berry, Leicester, in 1990.

53534, 20 June 1987

53534 (50534) rests outside Tyseley Depot following overhaul and repaint into BR blue and grey livery. Only around a dozen Class 104 cars carried this livery, and at the time 53534 was allocated to Old Oak Common. This Class 104 car was built by the Birmingham Railway Carriage & Wagon Company in 1958 and was scrapped by Mayer Newman, Snailwell, in 1991.

53539, 24 January 1987

53539 (50539) stands outside Tyseley Depot having been through a works overhaul, including a repaint into plain blue livery. 53539 was allocated to Cricklewood at the time, and was never allocated to Tyseley. This Class 104 car was built by the Birmingham Railway Carriage & Wagon Company in 1958 and would be scrapped by Gwent Demolition, Margam, in 1995.

53540, 20 October 1990
53540 (50540) arrives at London Paddington while carrying Network South East livery. Only four two-car sets received this livery, and were the final Class 104 cars in service. This Class 104 car was built by the Birmingham Railway Carriage & Wagon Company in 1958 and would be scrapped by Gwent Demolition, Margam, in 1995.

53614, 18 July 1990
53614 (50614) is seen making a station call at Southampton Central while carrying BR blue and grey livery. 53614 was allocated to Bristol Bath Road at the time, hence the 'B' set number. This Class 108 car was built by BR at Derby in 1958 and was scrapped by Mayer Newman, Snailwell, in 1991.

53617, 14 July 1990
53617 (50617) is seen waiting to depart from Weymouth with a working to Westbury.
This Class 108 car was built by BR at Derby in 1958 and would be scrapped by
Gwent Demolition, Margam, in 1992.

53652, 26 December 1985
53652 (50652) spends Christmas 1985 stabled at Tyseley carriage sidings while
carrying BR blue and grey livery. This Class 120 car was built by BR at Swindon
in 1958 and was scrapped by Mayer Newman, Snailwell, in 1987. None of these
distinctive units were saved for preservation, except for centre car 59276.

53688, 8 March 1986
53688 (50688) is seen carrying BR blue and grey livery while stabled at Tyseley
carriage sidings. 53688 had, on paper, been transferred to Ayr Depot in Scotland by
this date, but was still based in the Midlands. This Class 120 car was built by BR at
Swindon in 1958 and would be scrapped by Mayer Newman, Snailwell, in 1987.

53812, 27 September 1986
53812 (50812) is seen stabled at Tyseley Depot carrying plain blue livery. It is seen
coupled to long-time partner 53355. This Class 105 car was built by Cravens,
Sheffield, in 1958 and would be scrapped by Vic Berry, Leicester, in 1991.

53845, 14 March 1987

53845 (50845) rests in the spring sunshine at Tyseley carriage sidings. This had been transferred down from Ayr Depot two weeks previous, and would only last in service for another four months. This Class 116 car was built by BR at Derby in 1958 and would be scrapped by Vic Berry, Leicester, in 1988.

53867, 17 May 1986

53867 (50867) is seen at Tyseley carriage sidings while still retaining plain blue livery. 53867 had only just come to Tyseley from Stratford Depot, East London. This Class 116 car was built by BR at Derby in 1958 and would be scrapped by Vic Berry, Leicester, in 1988.

53870, 7 May 1988
53870 (50870) is seen stabled alongside the factory at Tyseley Depot carrying BR blue and grey livery, complete with Newton Heath set number on the front, as it was still allocated to the Manchester Depot at the time. This Class 116 car was built by BR at Derby in 1958 and was scrapped by Vic Berry, Leicester, in 1989.

53873, 21 February 1987
53873 (50873) is seen stabled outside the factory at Tyseley Depot carrying BR blue and grey livery, complete with Trans-Clyde logos. At this time Tyseley received a few Class 116 sets from Scotland, including 53873. This Class 116 car was built by BR at Derby in 1957 and was scrapped by M. C. Metals, Springburn, in 1992.

53876, 28 March 1987
53876 (50876) rests outside the factory at Tyseley Depot carrying BR blue and grey livery, complete with Trans-Clyde logos. 53876 would only last in service until the end of the year before being withdrawn. This Class 116 car was built by BR at Derby in 1957 and was scrapped by Vic Berry, Leicester, in 1988.

53888, 7 December 1985
53888 (50888) stands condemned at Tyseley Depot, having been stripped of spare parts, including windscreens and bogies. This Class 116 car was built by BR at Derby in 1958 and would be scrapped by Vic Berry, Leicester, in 1987.

53920, 12 July 1986
53920 (50920) is seen stabled at Tyseley carriage sidings while still carrying plain blue livery. This had recently come to Tyseley from Stratford Depot, and would be withdrawn still carrying this livery. This Class 116 car was built by BR at Derby in 1958 and was scrapped by Vic Berry, Leicester, in 1988.

53933, 13 June 1987
53933 (50933) is seen stabled on Tyseley Depot carrying BR blue and grey livery, complete with non-standard headlight. This Class 108 car was built by BR at Derby in 1960 and has been preserved at the Severn Valley Railway.

53939, 12 April 1986

53939 (50939, 977818) rests on Tyseley carriage sidings carrying BR blue and grey livery. When this car was withdrawn, it was taken into departmental service as a sandite car. This Class 108 car was built by BR at Derby in 1959 and was scrapped by Booth Roe Metals, Rotherham, in 1996.

53941, 21 June 1986

53941 (50941, 977836) is seen in the summer sun at Tyseley carriage sidings carrying BR blue and grey livery, complete with West Midlands logo. 53941 entered departmental service as a sandite car when it was withdrawn from passenger use. This Class 108 car was built by BR at Derby in 1959 and was scrapped by Booth Roe Metals, Rotherham, in 1996.

53970, 16 July 1988
53970 (50970) is seen stabled outside the factory at Tyseley Depot carrying BR blue and grey livery, complete with Newton Heath set number on the front. This two-car set was visiting Tyseley for tyre-turning on the wheel lathe, as it was not allocated to Tyseley until 1989. This Class 108 car was built by BR at Derby in 1959 and was scrapped by Gwent Demolition, Margam, in 1992.

53987, 26 April 1987
53987 (50987) is seen at Tyseley Depot having been split from its partner car, which was receiving attention on the wheel lathe. A lot of units used to visit Tyseley for tyre-turning, mainly from the Manchester area, including the Class 504 EMUs. This Class 108 car was built by BR at Derby in 1959 and was preserved at Peak Rail, but was later moved to the Midland Railway Centre, Butterley, who scrapped the car for spares in 1998.

54004, 6 June 1987
54004 (56004) is seen at Shirebrook in connection with the depot open day. 54004, along with partner 53045, carries SYPTE brown and cream livery, and this was the only two-car set to carry this attractive livery. This Class 114 car was built by BR at Derby in 1956 and was scrapped by Mayer Newman, Snailwell, in 1988.

54012, 2 April 1988
54012 (56012) is seen stabled at Tyseley Depot carrying BR blue and grey livery, complete with red bufferbeam. This Class 114 car was built by BR at Derby in 1956 and was scrapped by Mayer Newman, Snailwell, in 1991.

54052, 3 May 1986
54052 (56052) is seen stabled at Tyseley carriage sidings, unusually coupled to Class 127 Parcels car 55985. 54052 would only last another couple of months in service. This Class 101 car was built by Metro-Cammell, Birmingham, in 1957 and was scrapped by Vic Berry in 1986.

54057, 21 December 1985
54057 (56057) arrives at Birmingham New Street with a working from East Anglia, and was based at Cambridge at the time. This Class 101 car was built by Metro-Cammell, Birmingham, in 1957 and was scrapped by Mayer Newman, Snailwell, in 1988.

54081, 2 April 1988
54081 (56081) is seen stabled outside the factory at Tyseley Depot undergoing repairs, and awaits a new cab door to be fitted. This Class 101 car was built by Metro-Cammell, Birmingham, in 1957 and would be scrapped by Gwent Demolition, Margam, in 1994.

54086, 24 May 1987
54086 (56086) is seen condemned at Thornaby Depot showing signs of the collision damage it received after hitting HST car 43122 at Darlington Station. This Class 101 car was built by Metro-Cammell, Birmingham, in 1957 and was scrapped by Vic Berry, Leicester, in 1988.

54243, 9 May 1987
54243 (56243) is seen stabled on Tyseley Depot carrying BR blue and grey livery, and was allocated to Carlisle Kingmoor at the time. This Class 108 car was built by BR at Derby in 1959 and was scrapped by Booth Roe Metals, Rotherham, in 1992.

54257, 14 March 1987
54257 (56257) is seen at Tyseley carriage sidings having been split from its partner vehicle. 54257 still retains its First Class section at this time, and was about to transfer to Marylebone Depot, London. This Class 108 car was built by BR at Derby in 1959 and was scrapped by Gwent Demolition, Margam, in 1994.

54277, 16 May 1987
54277 (56277) is seen stabled inside the factory at Tyseley Depot carrying BR blue
livery. Of note is the old Merseyrail logo on the side, and this car still retains its
operational headcode boxes as late as 1987, despite them being obsolete since 1976.
This Class 108 car was built by BR at Derby in 1960 and was scrapped by Booth Roe
Metals, Rotherham, in 1991.

54281, 14 June 1986
54281 (56281, 977615) rests outside the factory at Tyseley Depot carrying BR
blue and grey livery. Upon withdrawal from passenger use, this car was taken into
departmental service as a sandite vehicle. This Class 121 car was built by Pressed
Steel, Paisley, in 1960 and would be scrapped by Vic Berry, Leicester, in 1990.

54443, 22 February 1986
54443 (56443) is seen stabled at Tyseley carriage sidings carrying plain blue livery, complete with 'not to be moved' board attached. This had arrived at Tyseley with a working from Norwich, and these services were due to be handed over to the Class 156 units. This Class 105 car was built by Cravens, Sheffield, in 1958 and was scrapped by Mayer Newman, Snailwell, in 1989.

54504, 15 August 2009
54504 (56504) is seen having been preserved at the Swanage Railway, and has been restored back to BR green livery. This Class 108 car was built by BR at Derby in 1960 and had originally been preserved at Peak Rail, Matlock.

54901, 10 August 1988

54901 (56016, 54016) is seen at Leeds having recently been converted for Parcels use, which included the addition of roller shutter doors, and the windows being plated over. This Class 114 car was built by BR at Derby in 1956 and was only in Parcels use for two years before being scrapped by M. C. Metals, Glasgow, in 1991.

54902, 2 April 1988

54902 (56036, 54036, 55932) is seen stabled at Tyseley Depot having been repainted into Royal Mail Parcels red livery. This Class 114 car was built by BR at Derby in 1957 and would be scrapped by M. C. Metals, Glasgow, in 1991.

55002, 14 December 1985

55002 rests outside the factory at Tyseley Depot carrying BR blue and grey livery. This Class 122 car was built by the Gloucester Railway Carriage & Wagon Company in 1958, and was scrapped by Vic Berry, Leicester, in 1987 having suffered collision damage at Coventry.

55005, 23 August 2016

55005 is seen at Shenton on the Battlefield Line, having been restored to BR blue and grey livery. This Class 122 car was built by the Gloucester Railway Carriage & Wagon Company in 1958. The Class 121 and Class 122 cars are known as bubble cars, due to them being just a single carriage, and quite a few are preserved.

55011, 4 January 1986
55011 is seen stabled at Tyseley carriage sidings carrying BR blue and grey livery, complete with 'not to be moved' board attached. This Class 122 car was built by the Gloucester Railway Carriage & Wagon Company in 1958 and was scrapped by Mayer Newman, Snailwell, in 1990.

55012, 22 February 1986
55012 (977941) is seen stabled at Tyseley carriage sidings carrying BR blue and grey livery. Upon withdrawal from passenger use, this entered departmental service as a route-learning car. This Class 122 car was built by the Gloucester Railway Carriage & Wagon Company in 1958 and has been preserved at the Weardale Railway.

55012, 16 March 1997
55012 (977941) is seen stabled at Thornaby Depot carrying Load Haul livery while in use as a route-learning car. This Class 122 car was built by the Gloucester Railway Carriage & Wagon Company in 1958 and has been preserved at the Weardale Railway.

55023, 10 July 2016
55023 is seen preserved at the Chinnor & Princes Risborough Railway having been restored to BR green livery. This Class 121 car was built by Pressed Steel, Paisley, in 1960 and has been based at Chinnor for nearly twenty years.

55024, 10 July 1986
55024 (977858) is seen preserved at the Chinnor & Princes Risborough Railway carrying maroon livery. This Class 121 car was built by Pressed Steel, Paisley, in 1960, and when it finished its passenger-carrying career it was converted to a sandite and route-learning car. It was preserved at Chinnor in 2013.

55027, 8 April 1989
55027 (977975) is seen stabled at Tyseley carriage sidings while carrying Network South East livery. This Class 121 car was built by Pressed Steel, Paisley, in 1960, and after finishing its passenger carrying duties it was taken into departmental use as a Severn Tunnel emergency train, but has since been preserved at the Ecclesbourne Valley Railway.

55028, 15 August 2009
55028 (977860) is seen preserved at the Swanage Railway having been beautifully
restored in BR green livery. This Class 121 car was built by Pressed Steel, Paisley,
in 1960 and was another bubble car to enter departmental service as a sandite and
route-learning car, before being preserved at Swanage.

55029, 23 June 2000
55029 (977968) *Marston Vale* is seen passing Washwood Heath while carrying
Silverlink livery while on route-learning duty. This Class 121 car was built by
Pressed Steel, Paisley, in 1960 and was converted into an inspection unit when it had
finished its passenger-carrying career. It has since been preserved at the Rushden
Transport Museum.

55031, 8 June 2000
55031 (977976) is seen passing Washwood Heath carrying Network South East livery while on a route-learning trip. This Class 121 car was built by Pressed Steel, Paisley, in 1960 and was named *Leslie Crabbe*. 55031 was converted to a Severn Tunnel emergency train and has now been preserved at the Ecclesbourne Valley Railway.

55032, 12 July 1986
55032 (977842) is seen stabled outside the factory at Tyseley Depot carrying BR blue and grey livery, complete with red lining from when it was allocated to Cardiff Canton. This Class 121 car was built by Pressed Steel, Paisley, in 1960 and would end up being preserved at the Wensleydale Railway.

55033, 7 June 1987

55033 (977826) is seen stabled at Tyseley Depot carrying its unique Midline livery. This Class 121 car was built by Pressed Steel, Paisley, in 1960, and when it finished its passenger-carrying career it was taken into the departmental fleet as a sandite unit. 55033 was finally preserved at the Colne Valley Railway.

55966, 8 April 1989

55966 (51591) is seen stabled at Tyseley carriage sidings carrying BR green livery. This had been converted to a Parcels carrying car in 1985. This Class 127 car was built by BR at Derby in 1959 and has been preserved at the Midland Railway Centre, Butterley, being rebuilt back into a passenger-carrying car.

55971, 28 June 1987
55971 (51597) rests at Tyseley carriage sidings carrying Red Star Parcels livery. This
was rebuilt as a newspaper carrying car in 1985. This Class 127 car was built by BR at
Derby in 1959 and would be scrapped by Vic Berry, Leicester, in 1991.

55985, 3 May 1986
55985 (51619) is seen stabled at Tyseley carriage sidings, unusually coupled to
Class 101 car 54052. This Class 127 car was built by BR at Derby in 1959 and was
scrapped by Vic Berry, Leicester, in 1991.

55993, 18 April 1986
55993 is seen stabled at Tyseley carriage sidings carrying Red Star parcels livery. This
Class 128 car was built by Gloucester Railway Carriage & Wagon Company in 1960,
and was one of six such vehicles built for Parcels work. 55993 was scrapped by M. C.
Metals, Glasgow, in 1991.

55994, 15 October 1988
55994 rests outside the factory at Tyseley Depot carrying Royal Mail Letters red
livery. There were three of these single-car Parcels cars allocated to Tyseley at this
time. This Class 128 car was built by the Gloucester Railway Carriage & Wagon
Company in 1960 and was scrapped by M. C. Metals, Glasgow, in 1991.

56062, 20 July 2006

56062 (54062) is seen making a station call at Weybourne on the North Norfolk Railway. This Class 101 car was built by Metro-Cammell, Birmingham, in 1957 and looks superb painted in plain blue livery.

56097, 20 September 2009

56097 stands in derelict condition at the Midland Railway Centre, Butterley. This Class 100 car was built by the Gloucester Railway Carriage & Wagon Company in 1957 and has been preserved since 1974.

56171, 26 March 2016

56171 (975006) is seen at Carrog on the Llangollen Railway having been superbly restored back to BR green livery. This Class 109 car was built by Wickham, Ware, in 1957, and after its passenger carrying days were finished, it was converted into an Eastern Region General Manager's Saloon, which would lead to its eventual preservation.

56333, 22 November 1981

56333 (54333) stands outside the factory at Tyseley Depot carrying refurbished white and blue livery. This Class 101 car was built by Metro-Cammell, Birmingham, in 1958 and was based at Chester Depot at the time. 56333 would be renumbered 54333, and was scrapped by a private contractor at Red Bank carriage sidings, Manchester, in 1986.

78959, 1 September 1987
78959 (50288, 53288) is seen at Leeds carrying BR blue and grey livery, complete with WYPTE MetroTrain logos. This Class 111 car was built by Metro-Cammell, Birmingham, in 1958 and was scrapped by Vic Berry, Leicester, in 1990.

79900, 18 June 2006
79900 (975010) is seen at the Midland Railway Centre, Butterley, having been restored to original condition, including a repaint into BR green livery. 79900 was last used as a test car, numbered 975010 and named *Iris*. This car was built by BR at Derby in 1956. It can today be found at the Ecclesbourne Valley Railway, and was known as a Derby Lightweight.

79960, 5 March 2016
79960 is seen preserved at the Ribble Steam Railway, looking very nice in original condition. This railbus was one of five built by Waggon und Masshienenbau in Germany in 1956, and today four out of the five survive.

79963, 30 August 2006
79963 is seen preserved at Mangapps Farm Railway. This railbus was one of five built by Waggon und Masshienenbau in Germany in 1956, and today it can be found at the East Anglian Railway Museum.

975349, 18 August 1984

975349 (51116) is seen at Doncaster Station while in use as an Inspection Saloon. This Class 100 car was built by the Gloucester Railway & Carriage Company in 1957 and managed to survive until 1993, when it was scrapped by M. C. Metals, Glasgow.

975540, 26 June 1990

975540 (55016) is seen at Birmingham New Street carrying plain blue livery while on route-learning duty. This Class 122 car was built by the Gloucester Railway Carriage & Wagon Company in 1958 and was withdrawn from passenger use as long ago as 1975. It was scrapped by M. C. Metals, Glasgow, in 1993.

977052, 8 October 1988
977052 (56145) is seen stabled at Tyseley Depot carrying plain blue livery. This
Class 105 car was built by Cravens, Sheffield, in 1957 and was converted to a sandite
car in 1981. It would be scrapped by Mayer Newman, Snailwell, in 1991.

977126, 16 September 1986
977126 (56445) is seen outside Saltley Depot, Birmingham, while on route-learning
duty. This Class 105 car was built by Cravens, Sheffield, in 1958 and would be
scrapped by Mayer Newman, Snailwell, in 1990.

977694, 30 July 2016
977694 (50338, 53338) is seen preserved at Barry Island on the Barry Island Railway.
This Class 101 car was built by Metro-Cammell, Birmingham, in 1958, and was
heavily rebuilt for the departmental sector, being named *Laboratory 19, Iris II*. The
interior still retains technical equipment, and has also been fitted with Mk 2 seats
from former Gatwick Express coaches.

977860, 6 August 2000
977860 (55028) is seen stabled at Aylesbury carrying Network South East livery
while in use as a sandite car. This Class 121 car was built by Pressed Steel, Paisley, in
1960 and would later go on to be used by South West Trains as a route-learning car,
before finally being preserved at the Swanage Railway.